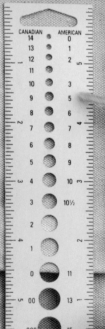

knit notes

explore • design • create

NADINE CURTIS

sixth&springbooks NEW YORK

contents

preface

I'm the owner of Be Sweet, a yarn company located in Sausalito, California, where I spend my days working with accomplished knitwear designers to develop designs that feature my yarns. Because creative inspiration can strike at a moment's notice, I've found that developing a project from inspiration to instruction can be an organizational challenge, even for the most experienced designer.

Therein lies the reason for creating *Knit Notes*: to give knitwear designers at all levels of skill and experience, from aspiring to seasoned, a place to document and develop the key elements of their projects. Having a structured template to sketch and refine ideas, record design details, and map a clear course for knitting a piece is essential to envisioning, realizing, and completing an original knitwear design. Careful documentation is an essential part of a knitter's successful evolution into a full-fledged designer, and an important component in creating beautiful designs supported by well-written—and ultimately marketable—patterns.

But this workbook isn't just for knitwear designers. It's for any knitter who wants to adapt an existing pattern to incorporate his or her own unique touches: change a color, substitute a fiber, recalculate measurements to improve fit, or add an edging or other unique detail.

I'm hopeful that *Knit Notes* will not only prompt you to keep track of the details that go into a well-designed knitted piece—perhaps one that someone else would like to knit—but will also encourage you to honor and refine your design process, and inspire you to enhance your creativity and transform your ideas into realities.

Love,

Nadine

inspiration

Where Design Begins

Inspiration for knitwear designs can come from anywhere and strike at any time. Sometimes they're developed to feature a specific yarn, fiber, color, or texture, while at others they're inspired by something a designer has seen or experienced, such as a fashion show, a trip to a flea market, or a visit to a park or a beach. Some projects are created specifically as gifts for loved ones.

Sometimes, though, it may be hard to get those creative juices flowing. If you're uncertain about how to begin, here are a few helpful prompts for getting started, along with some examples of garment and accessory designs.

YARN TASTING
• Design a piece using a fiber or blend you've never tried before, such as bamboo, baby mohair, or silk.
• Use an expensive yarn to design an accessory or small home decorating item that requires only one or two skeins.

YOUR PERSONAL TOUCH
• Adapt a pattern from your favorite knitwear designer by substituting the featured yarn with a different fiber or weight, or by changing the color or stitch pattern.
• Learn how to knit intarsia so you can enhance a simple garment with a colorwork motif of your own design.

THOUGHTFUL GIFTS
• As a surprise, design a scarf for your spouse to take on a trip.
• Using the team's colors as your starting point, design a collection of beanie hats, headbands, or wristers for your son's or daughter's sports team.

NATURE CALLS
• Use colors and textures found in nature to design a garment. Virtually any detail from the natural world— animals, plants, seascapes, or any landscape, even an urban one—can inspire a design. One of my most inspirational places is Clifton Beach in Cape Town, South Africa.
• Design whimsical booties or a hat-and-mitten set for your friend's newborn inspired by your favorite furry forest animal.

EXPRESS YOURSELF
• Let the lyrics of a song that moves you inspire a new design. How do the words make you feel—romantic, spiritual, feminine, sexy . . . ?
• Make a statement with your design about the things that you hold dear: your favorite color, pattern, musician, or sports team.

The possibilities are endless! ■

Sophie Kurnik used yarn made from recycled t-shirts in two bright, lively blues to create her Blue Bird Bucket Bag, which she named in honor of her yarn store.

Sue De Lara's lacy take on a basic rib, knit with bamboo yarn held double, gives the simple silhouette of her Nika tunic a unique touch.

A study in versatility and flowing elegance, this beautiful wrap cardigan, designed by Frances Becker of St. Francis Bay, South Africa, can be worn several ways.

Even food can inspire! Reminiscent of a challah bread, this stylish cowl was knit in strips that were then braided together. Designed by Tanis Gray.

Designer Tanis Gray was inspired by the fictional planet of Caprica from the television series *Battlestar Galactica* to create her stunning Caprica Shawl. The lace pattern mimics the planet's surface as seen from above, with its graceful skyscrapers, bodies of water, and open land.

how to use this book

As you can see, the ways in which a knitwear design can begin are virtually limitless. As you develop an idea, take the time to consider the following, all of which can be documented in the templates (see opposite for an example):

1 Think about why you're creating the project. Who (or what) is your inspiration? Whom do you see wearing or using it?

2 Collect any visual reference—an image torn from a magazine, paint chips for color ideas, bits of yarn—that you find inspiring.

3 4 Note the tools and materials—yarn, needles, and other notions—you'll need to create your piece.

5 Document any embellishments—buttons, zippers, or trims—that you would like to include.

6 7 Once you've created a swatch, record the stitch and row gauges for your chosen yarn.

8 This graph paper can be used to create a schematic drawing. A schematic drawing is made to scale and shows flat pieces before finishing and without selvages. To draw a schematic, use the grid as if each small square equals 1"/2.5cm. You can also use this area to sketch your design idea—its silhouette, some of its details, or both. Note that at the back of the book is a separate section of graph paper for charting colorwork and complex stitch patterns (see page 128).

9 Jot down all measurements, both of the finished piece and its intended recipient.

10 Record the instructions for the featured stitch pattern.

11 Take notes on the step-by-step process you used to create your design.

12 Attach a photo of the completed piece. (Once you've realized your vision, be sure to share a photo of your design and its pattern online.) Congratulations!

In addition to chart graph paper, at the back of the book you'll find helpful information for planning a knitwear design and writing or adapting a pattern, including common abbreviations, basic sweater and armhole shapes, standard measurements, worksheets for taking measurements, yarn substitutions and requirements for various projects, and the complete pattern for the garment shown opposite (for inspiration or for adapting into something new), plus a ruler printed on the inside back cover. ■

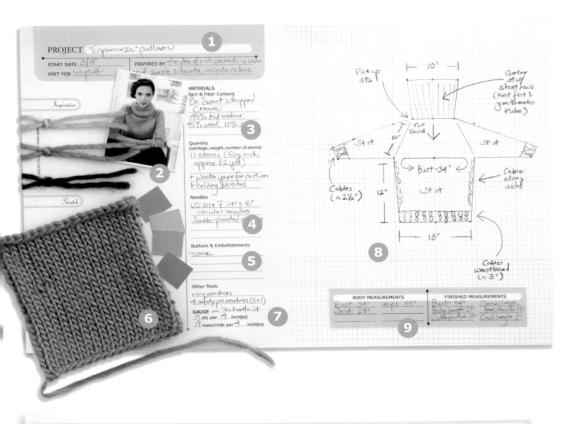

PROJECT "Esperanza" pullover — 1

START DATE 2/15
KNIT FOR myself!

INSPIRED BY the idea of rich warmth, a lush ... and simple silhouette, delicate cables

Inspiration — 2

Swatch

MATERIALS — 3

Yarn & Fiber Content
Be Sweet Whipped Cream
45% kid mohair,
45% wool, 10% s...

Quantity
(yardage, weight, number of skeins)
11 skeins (50g each,
approx 82 yds)
+ waste yarn for cast-on
& holding stitches

Needles — 4
US size 7 24" & 16"
circular needles
double-pointed ...

Buttons & Embellishments — 5
none

Other Tools — 7
ring markers
4 safety pin markers (3+1)
GAUGE in Stockinette st.
19 sts per 4 inch(es)
19 rows/rnds per 4 inch(es)

6

8

Pick up sts

10"

Garter stud short rows (Knit flat & join to make tube)

St st · Top Down ↓ · 10" · St st

Cables (~ 2½") · 12" · Bust ~34" · St st · Cable along sides

13"

Cable waistband (~3")

BODY MEASUREMENTS
Bust: 34" Hips: 35"
Waist: 29"

FINISHED MEASUREMENTS — 9
Bust: 34" Sleeve length ...
Body length 27" front shoulder 19"
Waist solution 13" Cowl length 2"

Pattern Notes "Esperanza" pullover

Stitch Pattern — 10
• Garter in Stockinette
• Cable
Rnd 1: * K2, p2, rep from * around — rep twice more
Cable rnd: * C2F, p2, rep from * around.
Rep last 4 rnds to desired length.

COLLAR
Prov c-o 30 sts. Work 16 rows in garter st. Short row K 20 sts, w/r, K next row. Work 16 rows in garter st. Rep short rows 16 plain rows till piece measures 19" along shorter side. Cut yarn, lvg 35" tail. Undo prov cast-on. Put sts on spare needle. Use kitchener stitch to connect 2 collar ends to form a tube.

BODY — 11
P.U. 72 sts along shorter edge of collar. PM for beg of rnd. Work 4 rnds in St st. PM — unique marker in 1st st (beg of rnd), then others in 10th, 37th & 46th sts. Remove marker @ beg of round.
* Shoulder shaping: Inc rnd: K 1st marker st, m1, k to 2nd marked st, m1, k marked st, m1, k to 3rd marker, m1, k marked st, m1, k to 4th marker, m1, k marked st, m1, k to end of round, m1 — 8 sts increased. K 1 rnd. Rep last 2 rnds 20 times more — 240 sts total. Work even till yoke meas. 10" along ne line. * Divide arms & body: K 1st round/marked st * Clip next 50 sts to waste yarn to ... sts later. Invisible Cast-on 12 sts. K across marked st. Rep from * to * once more. PM for beg of round — 164 st total. Knit 1 rnd plain. Next round: K3, p1, K4, p1, K76, p1, K4, p1, K to end. Work as

set for 6 rounds more. Cable round: K3, p1, C4F, p1, K76, p1, C4F, p1, K to end. Work 7 rounds as set. Rep last 8 rounds till piece meas. 10" from underarm.
* Border: Round 1: *K2, p2; rep from * around. Repeat Rnd 1 twice more. Cable round * C2F, p2, rep from * around. Rep last 4 rnds ...der meas. 2¾" or des. length. Bo loosely.

SLEEVES
Pu 50 sleeve sts from waste yarn & 13 sts from inv. c-o — 63 sts. Shift so ctr st along u'arm is beg of rnd. PM. Attach yarn & work around for 1". Dec rnd: K 1st st, ssk, k to last ... sts, K2tog. K 6 rnds. Rep last 7 rnds 6 more — 49 sts. Next rnds: k to end w/out dec. K2tog — 48 sts * K2 p2, rep ... Rep twice more ... round: * C2 ... * around ...

12

FINISH
Weave in ends w...

PROJECT

START DATE _____   INSPIRED BY _____

KNIT FOR _____   _____

Inspiration

PUNCH HOLES TO ATTACH YARN SAMPLES

Swatch

MATERIALS

Yarn & Fiber Content

Mystery
Mohair
double-Stranded

Quantity
(yardage, weight, number of skeins)

Needles

plate 1

Buttons & Embellishments

Other Tools

GAUGE

3 sts per 1 inch(es)

24 rows/rnds per 3 inch(es)

8/1"

even

every other

3"

13"

20"

3 4"

184 rows

120
3/4 rows

15" / rows

66 st

12 st
18
3 st

B10

30 st

2 4"
#13
rows

19" of
inc
= 152 rows

150 rows

20.25"
= 60 st
+1" either side
for roll

9

90 rows = every
other A = 495?

57 inc
70 rows = side
every 4th row
inc

22"
= 66

BODY MEASUREMENTS

FINISHED MEASUREMENTS

Stitch Pattern

~~M~~ 9

C/O 20 st
Inc every other row
on neck edge for ~~80~~
~~rows (20 st)~~ ~~142 rows~~
102 rows (60)

~~C/O 9 st~~ third
inc every other
row neck edge ~~past 53~~ rows
(60 st)
work ~~30 31~~ 80 row(s) even

C/O 9 - 2 rows even
inc 1 every other row
@ neck edge to 60 st
(114 rows) ~~#~~
78 ~~300~~ rows even

Knit 22, B/O 30, knit 14
Knit across next row - casting on
over bound off stitches

120
Knit ~~36~~ rows even

work second armhole like first

work 78 rows even
work decreases in reverse down
        9
to two rows even
    B/O

PHOTO
of completed
project

PROJECT **Machine Knit Socks**

START DATE _____

INSPIRED BY _____

KNIT FOR _____

Inspiration

PUNCH HOLES TO ATTACH YARN SAMPLES

Swatch

MATERIALS
Yarn & Fiber Content

Lana Grossa
Merino
80/20
Merino/Poly

Quantity
(yardage, weight, number of skeins)

100g / 420m

Needles

Buttons & Embellishments

Other Tools

GAUGE
_____ sts per _____ inch(es)

_____ rows/rnds per _____ inch(es)

BODY MEASUREMENTS

FINISHED MEASUREMENTS

Stitch Pattern

Cuff tension on 0
20 rows

stock - tension
main - 4
ribber - 6

even for 130 rows
(65 rounds)

turn heel (down to 10)

Foot   knit to   190 (95 rounds)

C/O ~~34~~ 65 st   too ↑ tight
Cuff 8+2 ~~on~~ ~~272~~... 1x1 dec down to 64
Main - 5   foot to ~~170~~ 138
Ribber - 7

Cuff - 20 rows
Ankle - ~~170 rows~~ (55 rounds) 100 rows (50 rounds)
Heel - down to 10
foot - 138 rows (69 rounds)
toe - down to 10

PHOTO
of completed
project

PROJECT *Baby Sweater*

START DATE _____ INSPIRED BY _____

KNIT FOR M & A'S Baby #2   3mo size

Inspiration

PUNCH HOLES TO ATTACH YARN SAMPLES

Swatch

MATERIALS
Yarn & Fiber Content

Cascade 220
Superwash

Quantity
(yardage, weight, number of skeins)

Needles

Buttons & Embellishments

Other Tools

GAUGE
_____ sts per _____ inch(es)

_____ rows/rnds per _____ inch(es)

BODY MEASUREMENTS

CHEST- 19"   Armhole depth - 3.25"
Sleeve Length - to underarm 6"   Cross-back - 7 1/4
Upper Arm - 5 1/2"

FINISHED MEASUREMENTS

_____   _____
_____   _____
_____   _____

Pattern Notes

Stitch Pattern

PHOTO
of completed
project

PROJECT

START DATE_____   INSPIRED BY_____

KNIT FOR_____

Inspiration

PUNCH HOLES TO ATTACH YARN SAMPLES

Swatch

MATERIALS
Yarn & Fiber Content

_____
_____
_____
_____
_____

Quantity
(yardage, weight, number of skeins)

_____
_____
_____
_____
_____

Needles

_____
_____
_____
_____
_____

Buttons & Embellishments

_____
_____
_____
_____

Other Tools

_____
_____

GAUGE
_____ sts per _____ inch(es)

_____ rows/rnds per _____ inch(es)

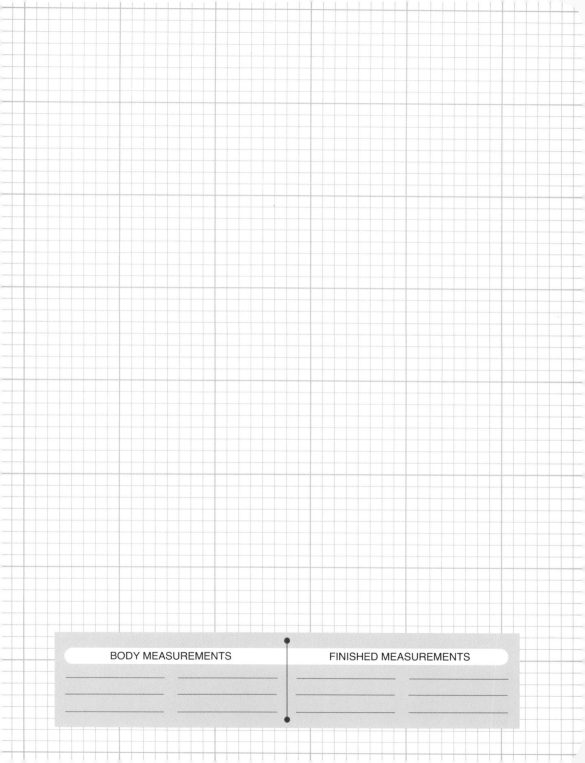

BODY MEASUREMENTS

FINISHED MEASUREMENTS

_____   _____   _____   _____
_____   _____   _____   _____
_____   _____   _____   _____

Pattern Notes

Stitch Pattern

PHOTO
of completed
project

PROJECT

START DATE_____ | INSPIRED BY_____

KNIT FOR_____ | _____

Inspiration

PUNCH HOLES TO ATTACH YARN SAMPLES

Swatch

MATERIALS
Yarn & Fiber Content

_____
_____
_____
_____
_____

Quantity
(yardage, weight, number of skeins)

_____
_____
_____
_____
_____

Needles

_____
_____
_____
_____
_____

Buttons & Embellishments

_____
_____
_____
_____

Other Tools

_____
_____

GAUGE
_____ sts per _____ inch(es)
_____ rows/rnds per _____ inch(es)

BODY MEASUREMENTS

FINISHED MEASUREMENTS

_____ _____

_____ _____

_____ _____

_____ _____

_____ _____

_____ _____

Pattern Notes

Stitch Pattern

PHOTO
of completed
project

PROJECT

START DATE_____

KNIT FOR_____

INSPIRED BY_____

_____

Inspiration

Swatch

MATERIALS
Yarn & Fiber Content

_____
_____
_____
_____
_____

Quantity
(yardage, weight, number of skeins)

_____
_____
_____
_____
_____

Needles

_____
_____
_____
_____
_____

Buttons & Embellishments

_____
_____
_____
_____
_____

Other Tools

_____
_____
_____

GAUGE
____ sts per____ inch(es)
____ rows/rnds per____ inch(es)

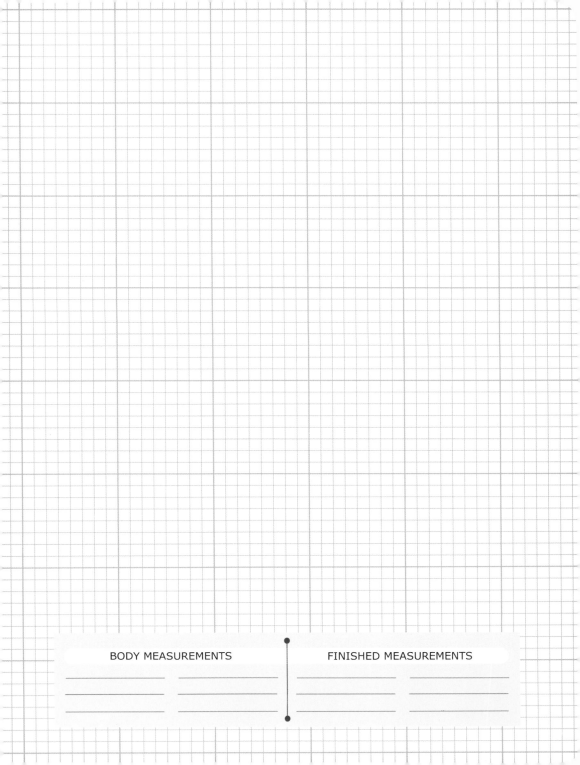

BODY MEASUREMENTS

FINISHED MEASUREMENTS

Stitch Pattern

PHOTO
of completed
project

PROJECT

START DATE_____   INSPIRED BY_____

KNIT FOR_____   _____

PUNCH HOLES TO ATTACH YARN SAMPLES

Swatch

MATERIALS
Yarn & Fiber Content

_____
_____
_____
_____
_____

Quantity
(yardage, weight, number of skeins)

_____
_____
_____
_____
_____

Needles

_____
_____
_____
_____
_____

Buttons & Embellishments

_____
_____
_____
_____

Other Tools

_____
_____

GAUGE
_____ sts per _____ inch(es)
_____ rows/rnds per _____ inch(es)

BODY MEASUREMENTS

_____   _____

_____   _____

_____   _____

FINISHED MEASUREMENTS

_____   _____

_____   _____

_____   _____

Pattern Notes

Stitch Pattern

PHOTO
of completed
project

PROJECT

START DATE_____

INSPIRED BY_____

KNIT FOR_____

Inspiration

PUNCH HOLES TO ATTACH YARN SAMPLES

Swatch

MATERIALS
Yarn & Fiber Content

_____
_____
_____
_____
_____

Quantity
(yardage, weight, number of skeins)

_____
_____
_____
_____
_____

Needles

_____
_____
_____
_____
_____

Buttons & Embellishments

_____
_____
_____
_____

Other Tools

_____
_____

GAUGE
_____ sts per _____ inch(es)

_____ rows/rnds per _____ inch(es)

BODY MEASUREMENTS

_____   _____

_____   _____

_____   _____

FINISHED MEASUREMENTS

_____   _____

_____   _____

_____   _____

Pattern Notes

Stitch Pattern

PHOTO
of completed
project

PROJECT

START DATE _____   INSPIRED BY _____

KNIT FOR _____   _____

Inspiration

Swatch

MATERIALS
Yarn & Fiber Content

_____
_____
_____
_____
_____

Quantity
(yardage, weight, number of skeins)

_____
_____
_____
_____
_____

Needles

_____
_____
_____
_____
_____

Buttons & Embellishments

_____
_____
_____
_____

Other Tools

_____
_____
_____

GAUGE
_____ sts per _____ inch(es)

_____ rows/rnds per _____ inch(es)

BODY MEASUREMENTS

_____   _____

_____   _____

_____   _____

FINISHED MEASUREMENTS

_____   _____

_____   _____

_____   _____

Pattern Notes

Stitch Pattern

PHOTO
of completed
project

PROJECT

START DATE_____   INSPIRED BY_____
                                                 _____
KNIT FOR_____

Inspiration

Swatch

MATERIALS
Yarn & Fiber Content

_____
_____
_____
_____
_____

Quantity
(yardage, weight, number of skeins)

_____
_____
_____
_____
_____

Needles

_____
_____
_____
_____
_____

Buttons & Embellishments

_____
_____
_____
_____

Other Tools

_____
_____

GAUGE
_____ sts per _____ inch(es)
_____ rows/rnds per _____ inch(es)

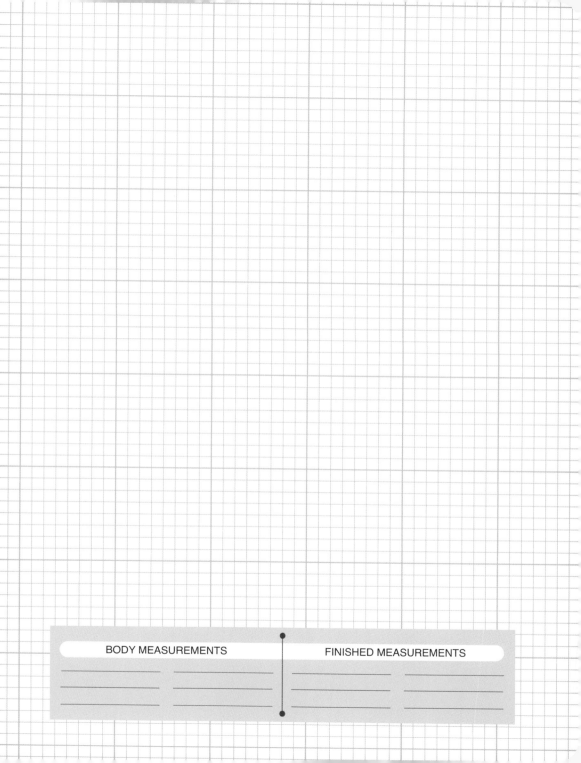

BODY MEASUREMENTS

FINISHED MEASUREMENTS

_____   _____   _____   _____

_____   _____   _____   _____

_____   _____   _____   _____

Pattern Notes

Stitch Pattern

PHOTO
of completed
project

PROJECT

START DATE_____ INSPIRED BY_____

KNIT FOR_____ _____

Inspiration

PUNCH HOLES TO ATTACH YARN SAMPLES

Swatch

MATERIALS
Yarn & Fiber Content

_____
_____
_____
_____
_____

Quantity
(yardage, weight, number of skeins)

_____
_____
_____
_____
_____

Needles

_____
_____
_____
_____
_____

Buttons & Embellishments

_____
_____
_____
_____

Other Tools

_____
_____

GAUGE
_____ sts per _____ inch(es)
_____ rows/rnds per _____ inch(es)

BODY MEASUREMENTS

FINISHED MEASUREMENTS

_____ _____   _____ _____
_____ _____   _____ _____
_____ _____   _____ _____

Stitch Pattern

PHOTO
of completed
project

PROJECT

START DATE_____   INSPIRED BY_____

KNIT FOR_____   _____

Inspiration

PUNCH HOLES TO ATTACH YARN SAMPLES

Swatch

MATERIALS
Yarn & Fiber Content

_____
_____
_____
_____
_____

Quantity
(yardage, weight, number of skeins)

_____
_____
_____
_____
_____

Needles

_____
_____
_____
_____
_____

Buttons & Embellishments

_____
_____
_____
_____

Other Tools

_____
_____

GAUGE
_____ sts per _____ inch(es)

_____ rows/rnds per _____ inch(es)

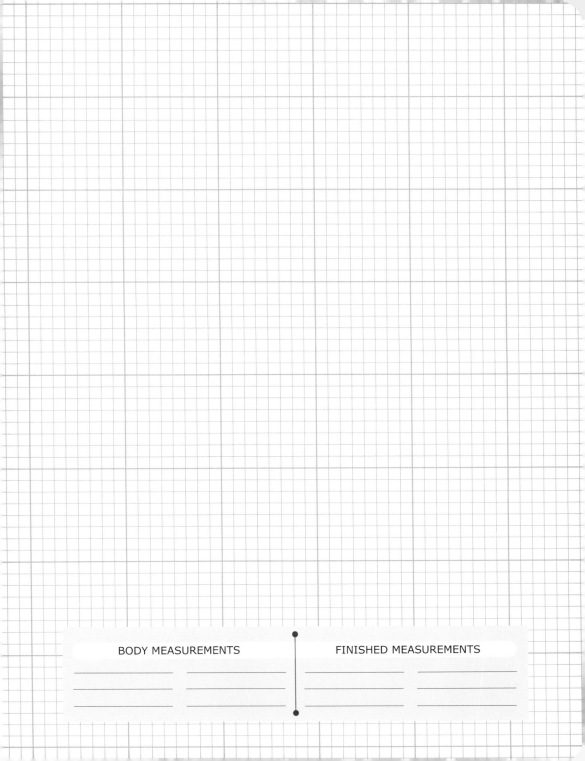

BODY MEASUREMENTS

FINISHED MEASUREMENTS

_____   _____

_____   _____

_____   _____

_____   _____

_____   _____

_____   _____

Stitch Pattern

PHOTO
of completed
project

PROJECT

START DATE _____   INSPIRED BY _____

KNIT FOR _____   _____

Inspiration

PUNCH HOLES TO ATTACH YARN SAMPLES

Swatch

MATERIALS
Yarn & Fiber Content

_____
_____
_____
_____
_____

Quantity
(yardage, weight, number of skeins)

_____
_____
_____
_____
_____

Needles

_____
_____
_____
_____
_____

Buttons & Embellishments

_____
_____
_____
_____

Other Tools

_____
_____

GAUGE
_____ sts per _____ inch(es)

_____ rows/rnds per _____ inch(es)

BODY MEASUREMENTS

FINISHED MEASUREMENTS

_____   _____   _____   _____

_____   _____   _____   _____

_____   _____   _____   _____

Pattern Notes

Stitch Pattern

PHOTO
of completed
project

PROJECT

START DATE_____   INSPIRED BY_____

KNIT FOR_____   _____

Inspiration

Swatch

MATERIALS
Yarn & Fiber Content

_____
_____
_____
_____
_____

Quantity
(yardage, weight, number of skeins)

_____
_____
_____
_____
_____

Needles

_____
_____
_____
_____
_____

Buttons & Embellishments

_____
_____
_____
_____

Other Tools

_____
_____

GAUGE
_____ sts per _____ inch(es)
_____ rows/rnds per _____ inch(es)

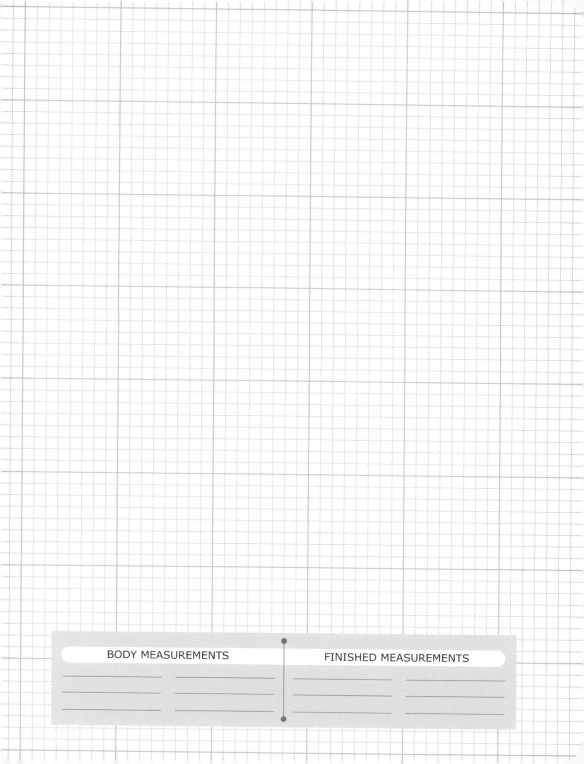

BODY MEASUREMENTS

FINISHED MEASUREMENTS

Pattern Notes

Stitch Pattern

PHOTO
of completed
project

PROJECT

START DATE_____

INSPIRED BY_____

KNIT FOR_____

Inspiration

PUNCH HOLES TO ATTACH YARN SAMPLES

Swatch

MATERIALS
Yarn & Fiber Content

_____
_____
_____
_____
_____

Quantity
(yardage, weight, number of skeins)

_____
_____
_____
_____
_____

Needles

_____
_____
_____
_____
_____

Buttons & Embellishments

_____
_____
_____
_____

Other Tools

_____
_____

GAUGE
_____ sts per _____ inch(es)
_____ rows/rnds per _____ inch(es)

BODY MEASUREMENTS

FINISHED MEASUREMENTS

_____ _____
_____ _____
_____ _____

_____ _____
_____ _____
_____ _____

Pattern Notes

Stitch Pattern

PHOTO
of completed
project

PROJECT

START DATE _____   INSPIRED BY _____
KNIT FOR _____   _____

Inspiration

Swatch

MATERIALS
Yarn & Fiber Content

_____
_____
_____
_____
_____

Quantity
(yardage, weight, number of skeins)

_____
_____
_____
_____
_____

Needles

_____
_____
_____
_____
_____

Buttons & Embellishments

_____
_____
_____
_____

Other Tools

_____
_____

GAUGE
_____ sts per _____ inch(es)
_____ rows/rnds per _____ inch(es)

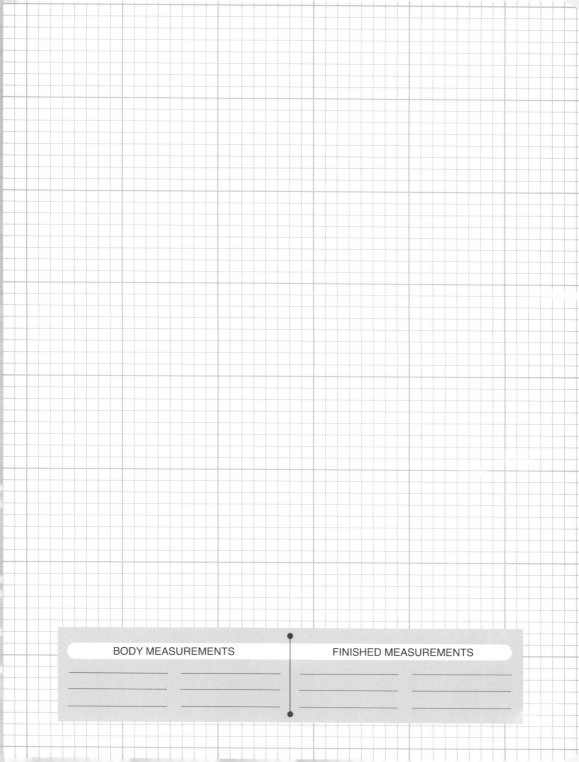

BODY MEASUREMENTS

FINISHED MEASUREMENTS

Pattern Notes

Stitch Pattern

PHOTO
of completed
project

PROJECT

START DATE_____   INSPIRED BY_____

KNIT FOR_____

Inspiration

Swatch

MATERIALS
Yarn & Fiber Content

_____
_____
_____
_____
_____

Quantity
(yardage, weight, number of skeins)

_____
_____
_____
_____
_____

Needles

_____
_____
_____
_____
_____

Buttons & Embellishments

_____
_____
_____
_____

Other Tools

_____
_____

GAUGE
_____ sts per _____ inch(es)

_____ rows/rnds per _____ inch(es)

BODY MEASUREMENTS   FINISHED MEASUREMENTS

_____   _____   _____   _____
_____   _____   _____   _____
_____   _____   _____   _____

Pattern Notes

Stitch Pattern

PHOTO
of completed
project

PROJECT

START DATE_____   INSPIRED BY_____

KNIT FOR_____   _____

Inspiration

Swatch

MATERIALS
Yarn & Fiber Content

_____
_____
_____
_____
_____

Quantity
(yardage, weight, number of skeins)

_____
_____
_____
_____
_____

Needles

_____
_____
_____
_____
_____

Buttons & Embellishments

_____
_____
_____
_____

Other Tools

_____
_____

GAUGE
_____ sts per _____ inch(es)
_____ rows/rnds per _____ inch(es)

BODY MEASUREMENTS

_____   _____

_____   _____

_____   _____

FINISHED MEASUREMENTS

_____   _____

_____   _____

_____   _____

Pattern Notes

Stitch Pattern

PHOTO
of completed
project

PROJECT

START DATE_____ INSPIRED BY_____

KNIT FOR_____ _____

Inspiration

PUNCH HOLES TO ATTACH YARN SAMPLES

Swatch

MATERIALS
Yarn & Fiber Content

_____
_____
_____
_____
_____

Quantity
(yardage, weight, number of skeins)

_____
_____
_____
_____
_____

Needles

_____
_____
_____
_____

Buttons & Embellishments

_____
_____
_____
_____

Other Tools

_____
_____

GAUGE
_____ sts per _____ inch(es)
_____ rows/rnds per _____ inch(es)

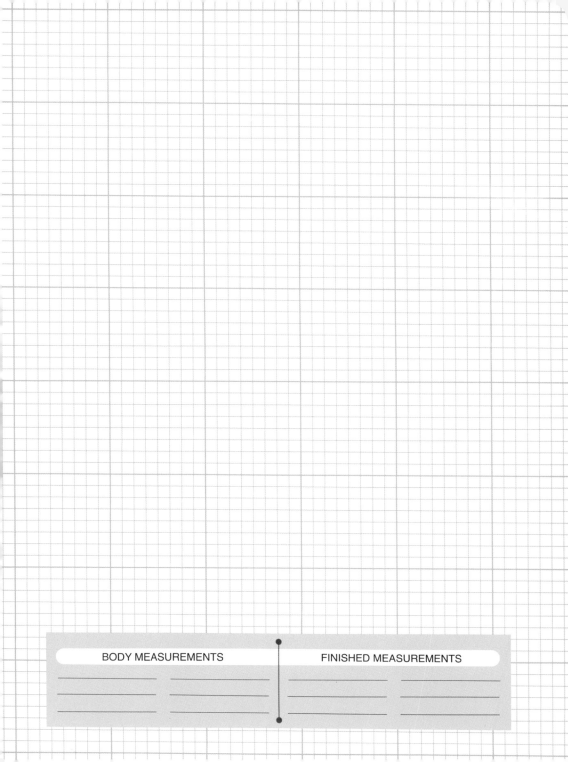

BODY MEASUREMENTS

FINISHED MEASUREMENTS

Pattern Notes

Stitch Pattern

PHOTO
of completed
project

PROJECT

START DATE_____

KNIT FOR_____

INSPIRED BY_____

_____

Inspiration

Swatch

MATERIALS
Yarn & Fiber Content

_____
_____
_____
_____
_____

Quantity
(yardage, weight, number of skeins)

_____
_____
_____
_____
_____

Needles

_____
_____
_____
_____
_____

Buttons & Embellishments

_____
_____
_____
_____

Other Tools

_____
_____

GAUGE
_____ sts per _____ inch(es)

_____ rows/rnds per _____ inch(es)

BODY MEASUREMENTS   FINISHED MEASUREMENTS

_____   _____   _____   _____
_____   _____   _____   _____
_____   _____   _____   _____

Pattern Notes

Stitch Pattern

PHOTO
of completed
project

PROJECT

START DATE_____

KNIT FOR_____

INSPIRED BY_____
_____

Inspiration

Swatch

MATERIALS
Yarn & Fiber Content

_____
_____
_____
_____
_____

Quantity
(yardage, weight, number of skeins)

_____
_____
_____
_____
_____

Needles

_____
_____
_____
_____
_____

Buttons & Embellishments

_____
_____
_____
_____

Other Tools

_____
_____

GAUGE
_____ sts per _____ inch(es)
_____ rows/rnds per _____ inch(es)

BODY MEASUREMENTS

_____   _____

_____   _____

_____   _____

FINISHED MEASUREMENTS

_____   _____

_____   _____

_____   _____

Pattern Notes

Stitch Pattern

Pattern Notes

PHOTO
of completed
project

PROJECT

START DATE_____   INSPIRED BY_____

KNIT FOR_____

Inspiration

Swatch

MATERIALS
Yarn & Fiber Content

_____
_____
_____
_____
_____

Quantity
(yardage, weight, number of skeins)

_____
_____
_____
_____
_____

Needles

_____
_____
_____
_____
_____

Buttons & Embellishments

_____
_____
_____
_____

Other Tools

_____
_____

GAUGE
_____ sts per _____ inch(es)

_____ rows/rnds per _____ inch(es)

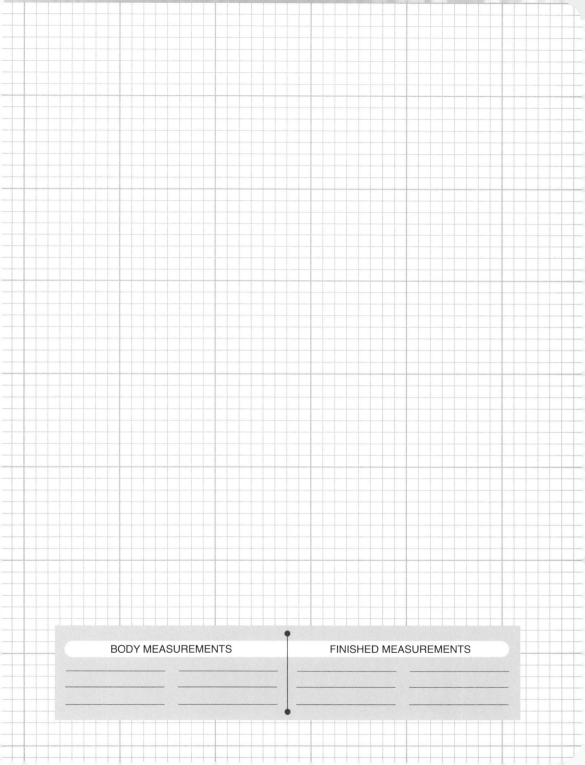

BODY MEASUREMENTS

FINISHED MEASUREMENTS

Stitch Pattern

PHOTO
of completed
project

PROJECT

START DATE _____   INSPIRED BY _____

KNIT FOR _____

Inspiration

PUNCH HOLES TO ATTACH YARN SAMPLES

Swatch

MATERIALS
Yarn & Fiber Content

_____
_____
_____
_____
_____

Quantity
(yardage, weight, number of skeins)

_____
_____
_____
_____

Needles

_____
_____
_____
_____
_____

Buttons & Embellishments

_____
_____
_____
_____

Other Tools

_____
_____

GAUGE
_____ sts per _____ inch(es)

_____ rows/rnds per _____ inch(es)

BODY MEASUREMENTS

_____   _____

_____   _____

_____   _____

FINISHED MEASUREMENTS

_____   _____

_____   _____

_____   _____

Pattern Notes

Stitch Pattern

Pattern Notes

PHOTO
of completed
project

PROJECT

START DATE_____

KNIT FOR_____

INSPIRED BY_____

_____

Inspiration

Swatch

MATERIALS
Yarn & Fiber Content

_____
_____
_____
_____
_____

Quantity
(yardage, weight, number of skeins)

_____
_____
_____
_____
_____

Needles

_____
_____
_____
_____

Buttons & Embellishments

_____
_____
_____
_____

Other Tools

_____
_____

GAUGE
_____ sts per _____ inch(es)

_____ rows/rnds per _____ inch(es)

BODY MEASUREMENTS

FINISHED MEASUREMENTS

_____   _____   _____   _____

_____   _____   _____   _____

_____   _____   _____   _____

Stitch Pattern

Pattern Notes

PHOTO
of completed
project

PROJECT

START DATE_____   INSPIRED BY_____

KNIT FOR_____

Inspiration

Swatch

MATERIALS
Yarn & Fiber Content

_____
_____
_____
_____
_____

Quantity
(yardage, weight, number of skeins)

_____
_____
_____
_____
_____

Needles

_____
_____
_____
_____
_____

Buttons & Embellishments

_____
_____
_____
_____

Other Tools

_____
_____

GAUGE
_____ sts per _____ inch(es)

_____ rows/rnds per _____ inch(es)

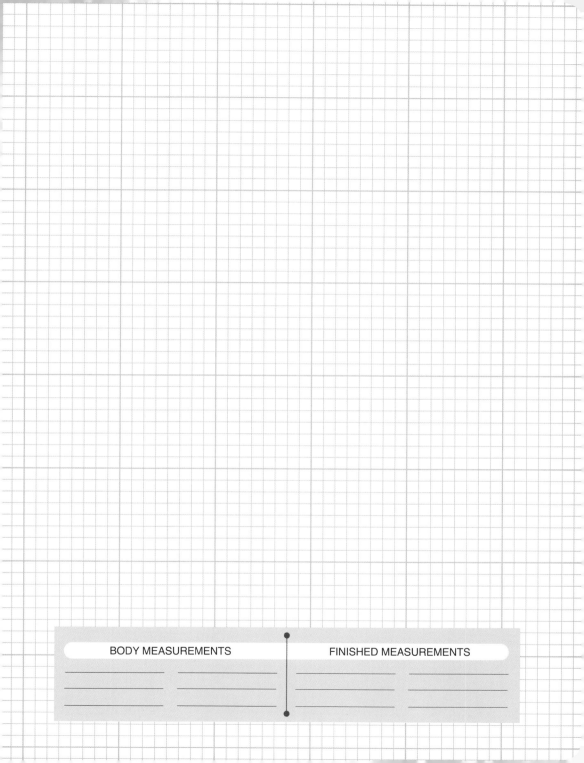

BODY MEASUREMENTS

FINISHED MEASUREMENTS

Pattern Notes

Stitch Pattern

PHOTO
of completed
project

PROJECT

START DATE_____   INSPIRED BY_____
KNIT FOR_____   _____

Inspiration

PUNCH HOLES TO ATTACH YARN SAMPLES

Swatch

MATERIALS
Yarn & Fiber Content

_____
_____
_____
_____
_____

Quantity
(yardage, weight, number of skeins)

_____
_____
_____
_____
_____

Needles

_____
_____
_____
_____
_____

Buttons & Embellishments

_____
_____
_____
_____

Other Tools

_____
_____

GAUGE
_____ sts per _____ inch(es)
_____ rows/rnds per _____ inch(es)

BODY MEASUREMENTS

FINISHED MEASUREMENTS

_____   _____   _____   _____
_____   _____   _____   _____
_____   _____   _____   _____

Pattern Notes

Stitch Pattern

PHOTO
of completed
project

PROJECT

Inspiration

PUNCH HOLES TO ATTACH YARN SAMPLES

Swatch

MATERIALS
Yarn & Fiber Content

_____
_____
_____
_____
_____

Quantity
(yardage, weight, number of skeins)

_____
_____
_____
_____
_____

Needles

_____
_____
_____
_____
_____

Buttons & Embellishments

_____
_____
_____
_____

Other Tools

_____
_____

GAUGE
____sts per ____ inch(es)
____rows/rnds per ____ inch(es)

BODY MEASUREMENTS

FINISHED MEASUREMENTS

_____   _____

_____   _____

_____   _____

_____   _____

_____   _____

_____   _____

Stitch Pattern

PHOTO
of completed
project

PROJECT

START DATE_____ INSPIRED BY_____

KNIT FOR_____ _____

Inspiration

Swatch

MATERIALS
Yarn & Fiber Content

_____

_____

_____

_____

_____

Quantity
(yardage, weight, number of skeins)

_____

_____

_____

_____

_____

Needles

_____

_____

_____

_____

_____

Buttons & Embellishments

_____

_____

_____

_____

Other Tools

_____

_____

GAUGE
_____ sts per _____ inch(es)

_____ rows/rnds per _____ inch(es)

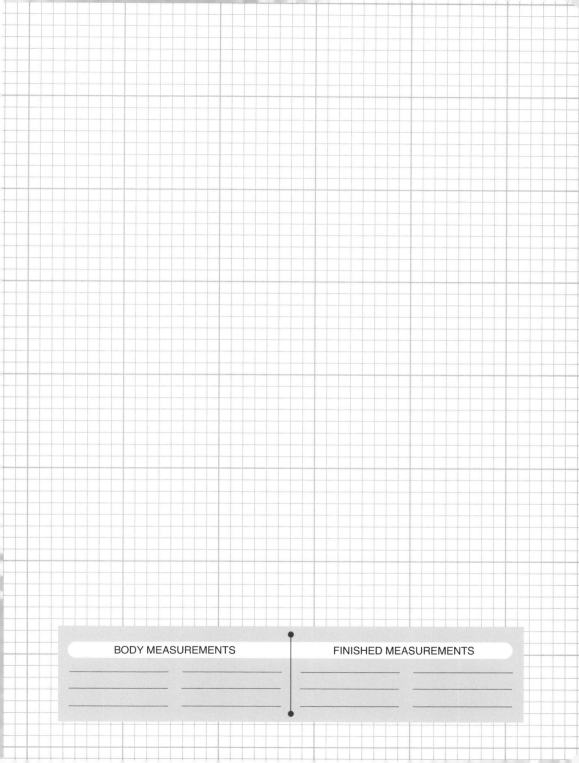

BODY MEASUREMENTS

FINISHED MEASUREMENTS

_____   _____   _____   _____
_____   _____   _____   _____
_____   _____   _____   _____
_____   _____   _____   _____

Pattern Notes

Stitch Pattern

PHOTO
of completed
project

PROJECT

START DATE_____   INSPIRED BY_____

KNIT FOR_____   _____

Inspiration

Swatch

MATERIALS
Yarn & Fiber Content

_____
_____
_____
_____
_____

Quantity
(yardage, weight, number of skeins)

_____
_____
_____
_____

Needles

_____
_____
_____
_____
_____

Buttons & Embellishments

_____
_____
_____
_____

Other Tools

_____
_____

GAUGE
_____ sts per _____ inch(es)
_____ rows/rnds per _____ inch(es)

BODY MEASUREMENTS

FINISHED MEASUREMENTS

_____   _____   _____   _____
_____   _____   _____   _____
_____   _____   _____   _____

Pattern Notes

Stitch Pattern

PHOTO
of completed
project

PROJECT

START DATE_____   INSPIRED BY_____

KNIT FOR_____

Inspiration

Swatch

MATERIALS
Yarn & Fiber Content

_____
_____
_____
_____
_____

Quantity
(yardage, weight, number of skeins)

_____
_____
_____
_____
_____

Needles

_____
_____
_____
_____
_____

Buttons & Embellishments

_____
_____
_____
_____

Other Tools

_____
_____

GAUGE
_____ sts per _____ inch(es)

_____ rows/rnds per _____ inch(es)

BODY MEASUREMENTS　　　　　　FINISHED MEASUREMENTS

_____ _____　　_____ _____

_____ _____　　_____ _____

_____ _____　　_____ _____

Stitch Pattern

Pattern Notes

PHOTO
of completed
project

chart graph paper

The graph paper in this section is scaled larger than the one in the templates so it's easier to document stitch patterns and colorwork. The list below shows standard symbols used by members of the Craft Yarn Council.

☐ K on RS, p on WS

▨ P on RS, k on WS

− P on RS, k on WS on a color chart

O Yarn over (yo)

⟋ K2tog on RS, p2tog on WS

⟋ P2tog on RS, K2tog on WS

⟍ SSK on RS, SSP on WS

⟍ SSP on RS, SSK on WS

⌐ Right-slanting inc

⌐ Left-slanting inc

V Sl 1 purlwise with yarn at WS of work

⋎ Sl 1 purlwise with yarn at RS of work

⟋3 K3tog on RS, p3tog on WS

⟍ SK2P, SSSK on RS, SSSP on WS

⋀ S2KP2 on RS, S2PP2 on WS

Ω K1 tbl on RS, p1 tbl on WS

Ω P1 tbl on RS, k1 tbl on WS

● Bobble

▉ Sts do not exist in these areas of chart (70% shade)

M Make 1 (M1) knitwise on RS, M1 purlwise on WS

M Make 1 (M1) purlwise on RS, M1 knitwise on WS

V Inc 1-to-3

V Inc 1-to-4

V Inc 1-to-5

⟋4 Dec 4-to-1 (right-slanting)

⟍4 Dec 4-to-1 (left-slanting)

⋀4 Dec 4-to-1 (vertical)

⟋5 Dec 5-to-1

℞ K1, wrapping yarn twice around needle

⌒ Bind off

2/1 **RPC** Sl 1 to cn, hold to back, k2; p1 from cn

2/1 **LPC** Sl 2 to cn, hold to front, p1; k2 from cn

2/2 **RC** Sl 2 to cn, hold to back, k2; k2 from cn

2/2 **LC** Sl 2 to cn, hold to front, k2; k2 from cn

2/2 **RPC** Sl 2 to cn, hold to back, k2; p2 from cn

2/2 **LPS** Sl 2 to cn, hold to front, p2; k2 from cn

2/1/2 **RPC** Sl 3 to cn, hold to back, k2; sl last st from cn to LH needle and purl it; k2 from cn

2/1/2 **LPC** Sl 3 to cn, hold to front, k2; sl last stitch from cn to LH needle and purl it; k2 from cn

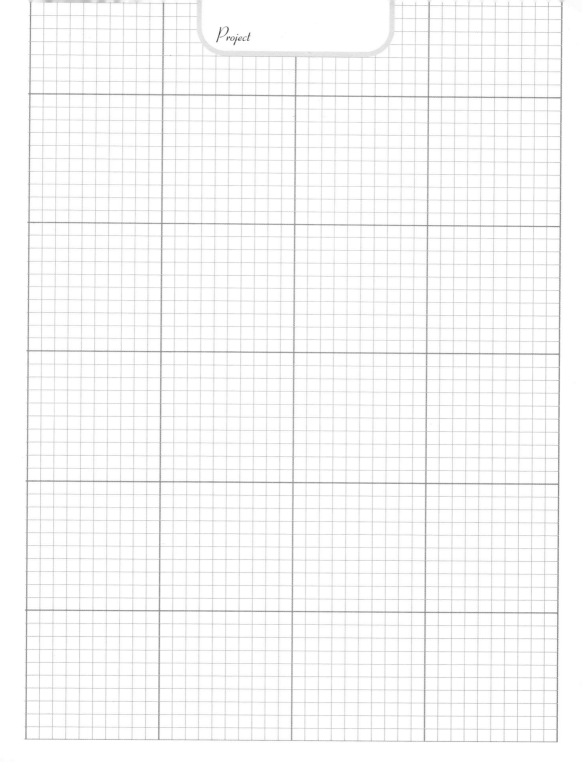

Project

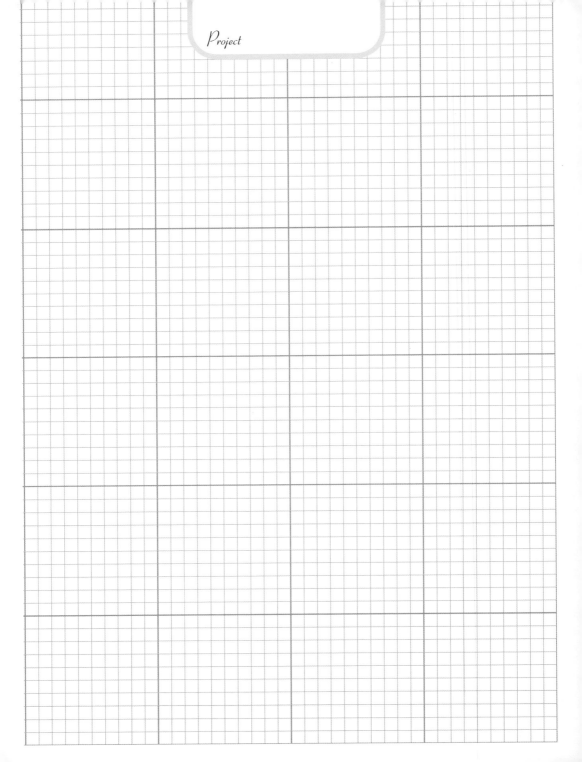

Project

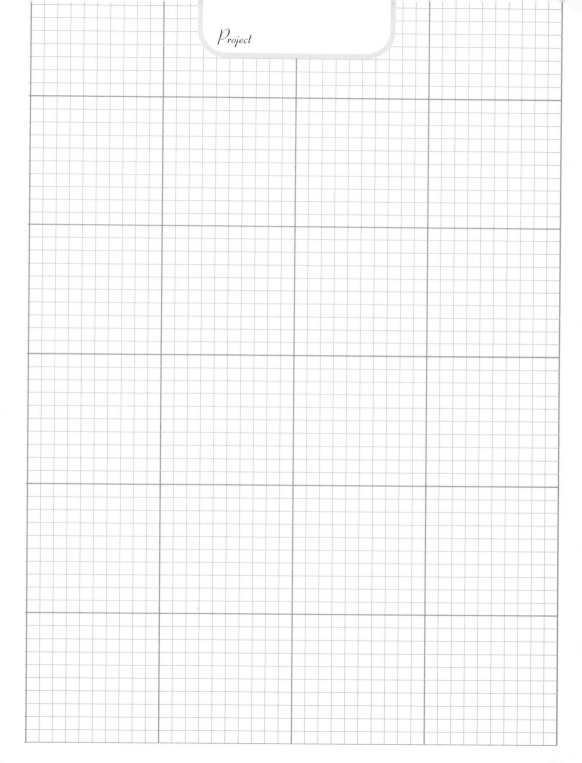

Project

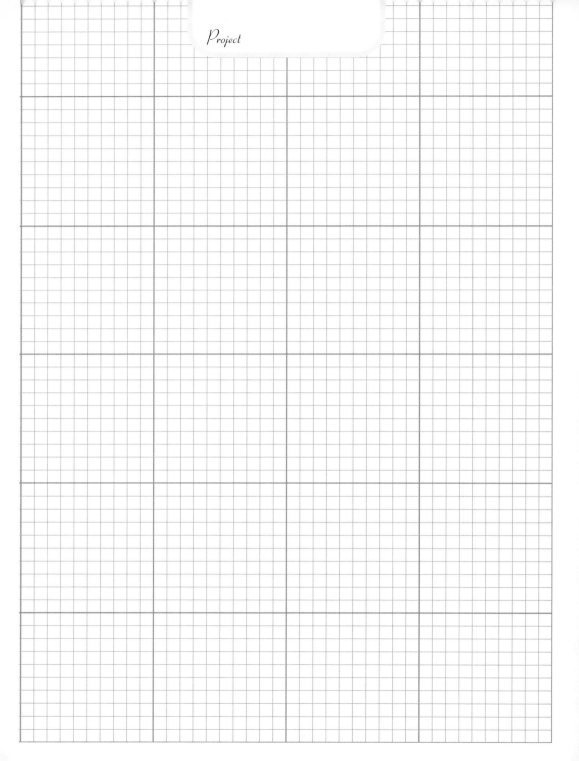

Project

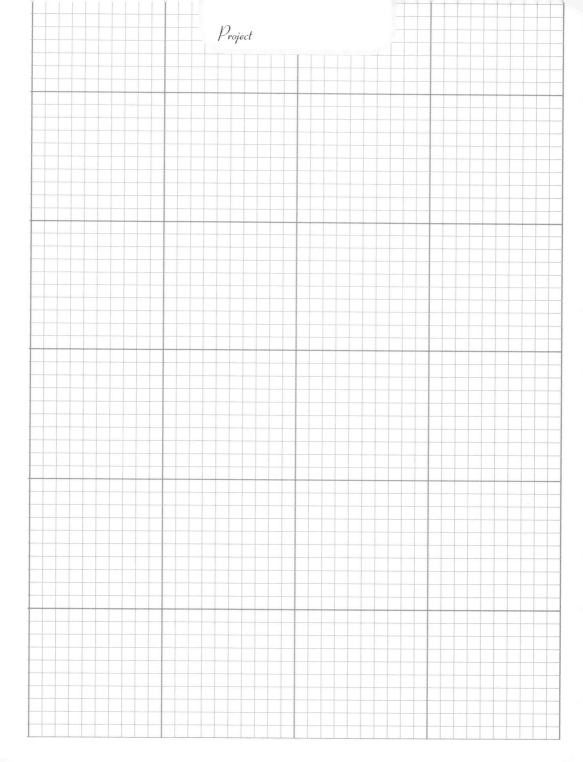

Project

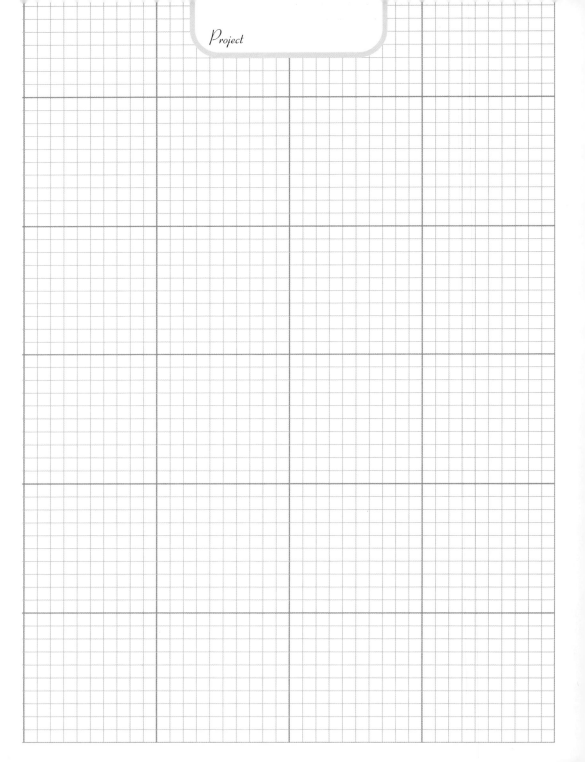

Project

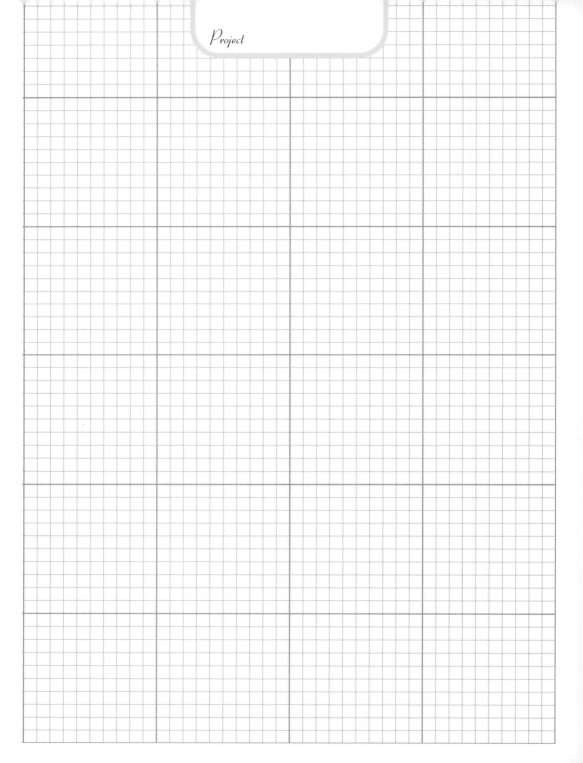

Project

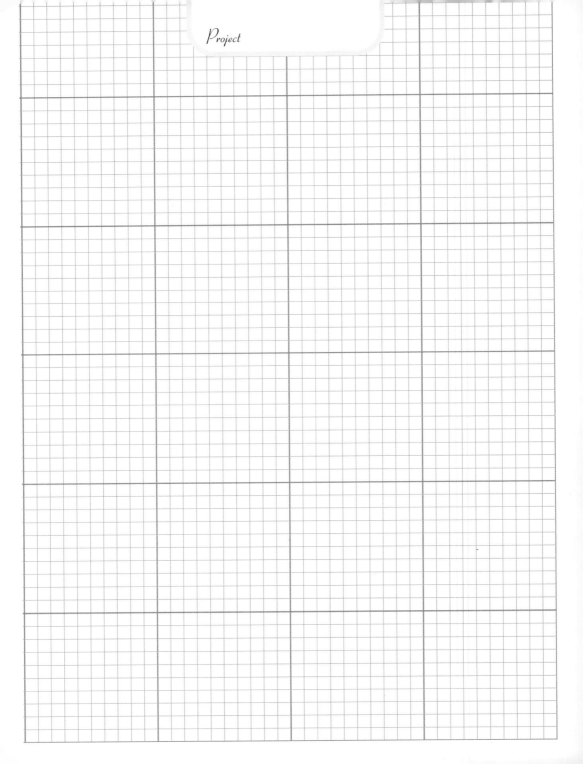

Project

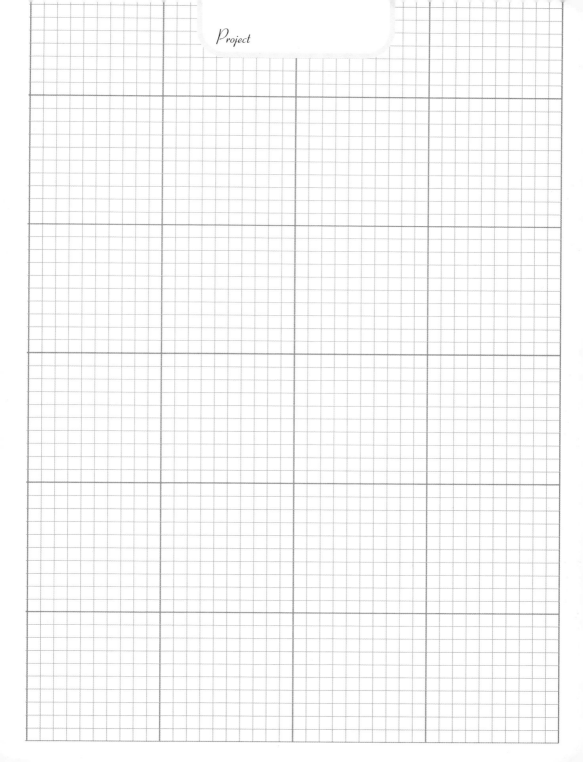

Project

designer essentials

This section provides information for designing knitwear and writing and adapting patterns.

common abbreviations

alt	alternate	**p1fb,**		**sl st**	slip stitch(es)	
approx	approximately	**p1f&b,**		**ssk**	slip two stitches	
beg	begin(s), beginning	**pfb**	purl into the front		knitwise one after	
bet	between		and back of a stitch		another, then knit	
bl	back loop(s)	**p2tog**	purl two stitches		these two stitches	
BO	bind off		together		together	
CC	contrasting color	**pat(s),**		**ssp**	slip two stitches	
ch	chain, chain stitch	**patt(s)**	pattern(s)		knitwise one after	
cm	centimeter(s)	**pm**	place marker		another, then purl	
cn	cable needle	**prev**	previous		these two stitches	
CO	cast on	**psso**	pass the slipped		together through the	
cont	continue(s), continuing		stitch over		back loop	
dec	decrease(s),decreasing	**pwise**	purlwise	**sssk**	slip three stitches	
dpn(s)	double-pointed needle(s)	**RC**	right cross		knitwise one after	
fl	front loop(s)	**rem**	remain(s), remaining		another, then knit	
foll	follow(s), following	**rep**	repeat(s), repeating		these three stitches	
g	gram	**rev**	reverse		together	
inc	increase(s), increasing	**rev**		**st(s)**	stitch(es)	
k	knit	**St st**	reverse stockinette stitch	**St st**	stockinette stitch	
k1-b,		**RH**	right-hand	**tbl**	through back loop(s)	
k-b	knit one stitch in row	**rib**	ribbing	**tog**	together	
	below	**rnd(s)**	round(s)	**WS**	wrong side	
k1fb,		**RS**	right side	**wyib**	with yarn in back	
k1f&b,		**s2kp**	slip two stitches	**wyif**	with yarn in front	
kfb	knit into the front and		together knitwise,	**yd**	yard(s)	
	back of a stitch; also		knit one stitch, pass	**yfwd**	yarn forward (same	
	called bar increase		the two slipped		as a yo)	
k2tog	knit two stitches		stitches over the knit	**yo, yon**	yarn over	
	together		stitch	*****	repeat the directions	
kwise	knitwise	**sc**	single crochet		between the	
LC	left cross	**sk**	skip		asterisks as many	
LH	left-hand	**sk2p**	slip one stitch, knit		times as indicated	
lp(s)	loop(s)		two stitches together,	******	repeat the directions	
m	meter(s)		pass the slipped stitch		between the double	
m1, M1	make one: increase		over the two stitches		asterisks as many	
	one stitch		knit together		times as indicated	
M1 p-st	make one purl stitch	**skp**	slip one stitch, knit	**[ ]**	work instructions	
MC	main color		one stitch, pass the		within brackets as a	
mm	millimeter(s)		slipped stitch over		group as many times	
oz	ounce(s)		the knit stitch		as indicated	
p	purl	**sl**	slip	**( )**	work instructions	
		sl1k,			within parentheses	
		sl 1k	slip one stitch knitwise		in the place directed	
		sl1p,				
		sl 1p	slip one stitch purlwise			

types of sweaters

This is an overview of some standard sweater styles, as determined by the armhole. The body can have more or less shaping, and the sleeve length can vary dramatically, but nothing changes the overall look of a sweater like the armholes.

❶ Straight Armhole/Drop Shoulder
This sleeve top has a straight edge that is sewn along the edge of the body pieces to form a T-square look. The width of the top of the sleeve is the total depth of the front and back armholes. Since the armhole isn't shaped, it should be dropped a minimum of 2½–3" (6.5–7.5cm) from the actual body measurement to ensure an easy, non-clinging fit.

❷ Square Armhole/Straight Sleeve
This sleeve is similar to the previous style, but has less bulk at the underarm. The average width to bind off for the armhole is 2" (5cm). You must work a corresponding 2" (5cm) straight at

the sleeve top after you complete all the sleeve increases.

❸ Angled Armhole/Sleeve
Very common in classic menswear and full-fashioned sweaters, this armhole shaping is often accompanied by a straight front shoulder and a deep, sloped back shoulder. It gives a broader line at the top of the sleeve without the bulk of a straight sleeve, and the angle gives more ease of movement.

❹ Shaped Armhole/Set-in Sleeve
The set-in sleeve is not only the most classic form of shaping, but offers numerous style possibilities, from a very shallow but broad cap to a very high but narrow cap. Set-in sleeves require careful

calculation and can be difficult to plan out. Puffed sleeves also fall into this category; they're deeper and wider at the top than a normal set-in sleeve, to allow for gathers.

❺ Raglan Armhole/Sleeve
A raglan armhole is usually seen as a straight line angled from the underarm to the neck. The sleeve raglan must match the front and back raglan shaping (they must have the same number of rows). Frequently, raglan decreases are worked 2 to 3 stitches inside each edge for a decorative finish, called full-fashioning.

❻ Saddle Yoke Armhole/Sleeve
The same principle for the set-in sleeve applies to the armhole and sleeve

of the saddle shoulder style. The only difference is that the front and back armholes are shorter by about 1" (2.5cm) to accommodate the saddle shoulder portion of the sleeve. The top of the saddle shoulder will also form part of the neck.

❼ Dolman Sleeve
The dolman sleeve has always been a classic shaping for evening sweaters and other lightweight dressy sweaters. Actually an extension of the main body pieces, the dolman is worked by increasing stitches, then casting on stitches in larger numbers to obtain the desired curve. It's important to plan the shaping with a graph or paper pattern.

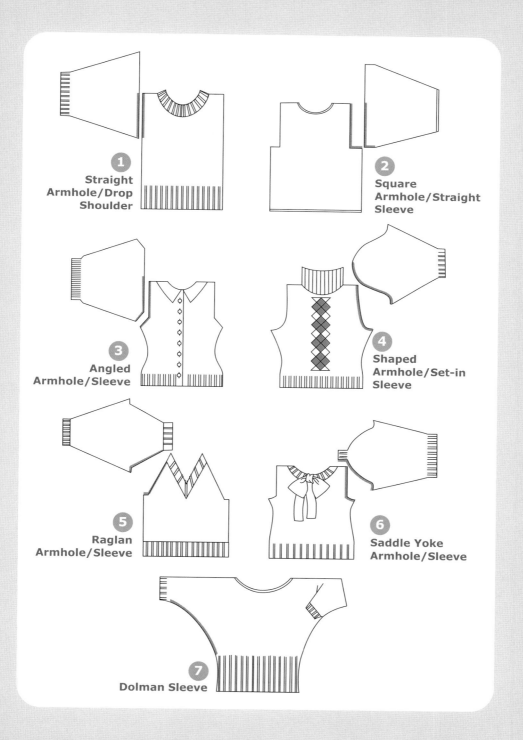

1 Straight Armhole/Drop Shoulder

2 Square Armhole/Straight Sleeve

3 Angled Armhole/Sleeve

4 Shaped Armhole/Set-in Sleeve

5 Raglan Armhole/Sleeve

6 Saddle Yoke Armhole/Sleeve

7 Dolman Sleeve

taking measurements

Whether you're designing your own garments or following a pattern, good fit starts with an accurate set of body measurements—and a good tape measure. If you're designing for yourself, you'll get a more accurate read if you enlist the help of a friend. Hold the tape snug (but not tight) as you record the measurements shown below.

❷ BUST
Measure around the fullest part of the chest, and don't let the tape slide down or up your back.

❸ WAIST
This measurement will help you determine the overall shape and silhouette of the garment. This is the narrowest point on your torso.

❹ HIPS
Measure your hips at their widest point below the waist.

❺ SHOULDER TO UNDERARM
Measure from the top of the shoulder to the underarm. This gives you the depth of the armhole.

❻ UPPER ARM
Measure around your upper arm at the widest point.

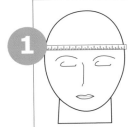

❶ HEAD
Place a tape measure across the forehead and measure around the full circumference of the head. Keep the tape snug for accurate results.

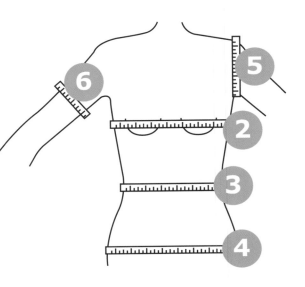

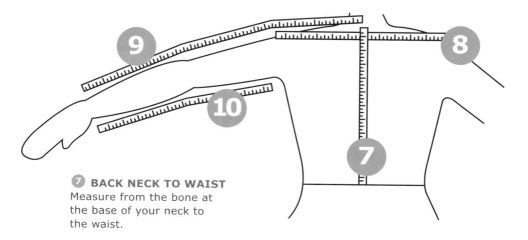

7 BACK NECK TO WAIST
Measure from the bone at the base of your neck to the waist.

8 CROSS BACK
Measure across the back from the tip of one shoulder to the other.

9 CENTER BACK NECK TO WRIST
With the arm extended, measure from the center bone at the back of the neck to the wrist bone, or to the point where you want the sleeve to end.

10 WRIST TO UNDERARM
With the elbow slightly bent, measure from the wrist bone along the underside of your arm to approximately 1"/2.5cm before the underarm.

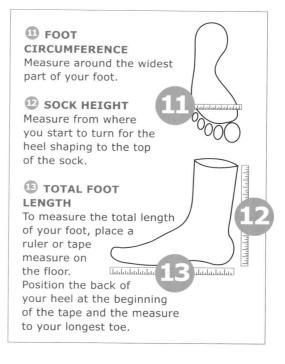

11 FOOT CIRCUMFERENCE
Measure around the widest part of your foot.

12 SOCK HEIGHT
Measure from where you start to turn for the heel shaping to the top of the sock.

13 TOTAL FOOT LENGTH
To measure the total length of your foot, place a ruler or tape measure on the floor. Position the back of your heel at the beginning of the tape and the measure to your longest toe.

standard measurements

These guidelines are adapted from the Craft Yarn Council's Standard Body Measurements/Sizing (YarnStandards.com).

WOMAN	X-Small	Small	Medium	Large	1X	2X	3X	4X	5X
BUST									
inches	28–30	32–34	36–38	40–42	44–46	48–50	52–54	56–58	60–62
cm	71–76	81–86	91.5–96.5	101.5–106.5	111.5–117	122–127	132–137	142–147	152–158
CENTER BACK NECK TO CUFF									
inches	27–27½	28–28½	29–29½	30–30½	31–31½	31½–32	32½–33	32½–33	33–33½
cm	68.5–70	71–72.5	73.5–75	76–77.5	78.5–80	80–81.5	82.5–84	82.5–84	84–85
BACK WAIST LENGTH									
inches	16½	17	17¼	17½	17¾	18	18	18½	18½
cm	42	43	43.5	44.5	45	45.5	45.5	47	47
CROSS BACK (SHOULDER TO SHOULDER)									
inches	14–14½	14½–15	16–16½	17–17½	17½	18	18	18½	18½
cm	35.5–37	37–38	40.5–42	43–44.5	44.5	45.5	45.5	47	47
SLEEVE LENGTH TO UNDERARM									
inches	16½	17	17	17½	17½	18	18	18½	18½
cm	42	43	43	44.5	44.5	45.5	45.5	47	47
UPPER ARM									
inches	9¾	10¼	11	12	13½	15½	17	18½	19½
cm	25	26	28	30.5	34.5	39.5	43	47	49.5
ARMHOLE DEPTH									
inches	6–6½	6½–7	7–7½	7½–8	8–8½	8½–9	9–9½	9½–10	10–10½
cm	15.5–16.5	16.5–17.5	17.5–19	19–20.5	20.5–21.5	21.5–23	23–24	24–25.5	25.5–26.5
WAIST									
inches	23–24	25–26½	28–30	32–34	36–38	40–42	44–45	46–47	49–50
cm	58.5–61	63.5–67.5	71–76	81.5–86.5	91.5–96.5	101.5–106.5	111.5–114	116.5–119	124–127
HIPS									
inches	33–34	35–36	38–40	42–44	46–48	52–53	54–55	56–57	61–62
cm	83.5–86	89–91.5	96.5–101.5	106.5–111.5	116.5–122	132–134.5	137–139.5	142–144.5	155–157

MAN	Small	Medium	Large	X-Large	XX-Large
CHEST					
inches	34–36	38–40	42–44	46–48	50–52
cm	86–91.5	96.5–101.5	106.5–111.5	116.5–122	127–132
CENTER BACK NECK TO CUFF					
inches	32–32½	33–33½	34–34½	35–35½	36–36½
cm	81–82.5	83.5–85	86.5–87.5	89–90	91.5–92.5
BACK HIP LENGTH					
inches	25–25½	26½–26¾	27–27¼	27½–27¾	28–28½
cm	63.5–64.5	67.5–68	68.5–69	69.5–70.5	71–72.5
CROSS BACK (SHOULDER TO SHOULDER)					
inches	15½–16	16½–17	17½–18	18–18½	18½–19
cm	39.5–40.5	42–43	44.5–45.5	45.5–47	47–48
SLEEVE LENGTH TO UNDERARM					
inches	18	18½	19½	20	20½
cm	45.5	47	49.5	50.5	52
UPPER ARM					
inches	12	13	15	16	17
cm	30.5	33	38	40.5	43
ARMHOLE DEPTH					
inches	8½–9	9–9½	9½–10	10–10½	10½–11
cm	21.5–23	23–24	24–25.5	25.5–26	26.5–28
WAIST					
inches	28–30	32–34	36–38	42–44	46–48
cm	71–76	81.5–86.5	91.5–96.5	106.5–112	117–122
HIPS					
inches	35–37	39–41	43–45	47–49	51–53
cm	89–94	99–104	109–114	119–124.5	129–134

SIZES

YOUTH	12	14	16
CHEST			
inches	30	31½	32½
cm	76	80	82.5
CENTER BACK NECK TO CUFF			
inches	26	27	28
cm	66	68.5	7
BACK WAIST LENGTH			
inches	15	15½	16
cm	38	39.5	40.5
CROSS BACK			
inches	12	12¼	13
cm	30.5	31	33
SLEEVE LENGTH TO UNDERARM			
inches	15	16	16½
cm	38	40.5	42
UPPER ARM			
inches	9	9¼	9½
cm	23	23.5	24
ARMHOLE DEPTH			
inches	6½	7	7½
cm	16.5	17.5	19
WAIST			
inches	25	26½	27½
cm	63.5	67.5	69.5
HIPS			
inches	21½	33	35½
cm	80	83.5	90

SIZES

CHILD	2	4	6	8	10
CHEST					
inches	21	23	25	26½	28
cm	53	58.5	63.5	67	71
CENTER BACK NECK TO CUFF					
inches	18	19½	20½	22	24
cm	45.5	49.5	52	56	61
BACK WAIST LENGTH					
inches	8½	9½	10½	12½	14
cm	21.5	24	26.5	31.5	35.5
CROSS BACK (SHOULDER TO SHOULDER)					
inches	9¼	9¾	10¼	10¾	11¼
cm	23.5	25	26	27	28.5
SLEEVE LENGTH TO UNDERARM					
inches	8½	10½	11½	12½	13½
cm	21.5	26.5	29	31.5	34.5
UPPER ARM					
inches	7	7½	8	8½	8¾
cm	17.5	19	20.5	21.5	22
ARMHOLE DEPTH					
inches	4¼	4¾	5	5½	6
cm	10.5	12	12.5	14.5	15.5
WAIST					
inches	21	21½	22½	23½	24½
cm	53.5	54.5	57	59.5	62
HIPS					
inches	22	23½	25	28	29½
cm	56	59.5	63.5	71	75

HEAD CIRCUMFERENCES

	PREEMIE	BABY	TODDLER	CHILD	WOMAN	MAN
inches	12	14	16	18	20	22
cm	30.5	35.5	40.5	45.5	50.5	56

SIZES

BABY	3 months	6 months	12 months	18 months	24 months
CHEST					
inches	16	17	18	19	20
cm	*40.5*	*43*	*45.5*	*48*	*50.5*
CENTER BACK NECK TO CUFF					
inches	10½	11½	12½	14	18
cm	*26.5*	*29*	*31.5*	*35.5*	*45.5*
BACK WAIST LENGTH					
inches	6	7	7½	8	8½
cm	*15.5*	*17.5*	*19*	*20.5*	*21.5*
CROSS BACK (SHOULDER TO SHOULDER)					
inches	7¼	7¾	8¼	8½	8¾
cm	*18.5*	*19.5*	*21*	*21.5*	*22*
SLEEVE LENGTH TO UNDERARM					
inches	6	6½	7½	8	8½
cm	*15.5*	*16.5*	*19*	*20.5*	*21.5*
UPPER ARM					
inches	5½	6	6½	7	7½
cm	*14*	*15.5*	*16.5*	*17.5*	*19*
ARMHOLE DEPTH					
inches	3¼	3½	3¾	4	4¼
cm	*8.5*	*9*	*9.5*	*10*	*10.5*
WAIST					
inches	18	19	20	20½	21
cm	*45.5*	*48*	*50.5*	*52*	*53.5*
HIPS					
inches	19	20	20	21	22
cm	*48*	*50.5*	*50.5*	*53.5*	*56*

FOOT SIZES

SHOE SIZE		FOOT CIRCUMFERENCE		SOCK HEIGHT		TOTAL FOOT LENGTH	
		inches	cm	inches	cm	inches	cm
CHILD	0–4	4½	11	2½	6.5	4	10
	4–8	5½	14	3½	9	5	13
	7–11	6	15.5	4½	11.5	6	15.5
	10–2	6½	16.5	5½	14	7½	19
	2–6	7	17.5	6½	16.5	8	20.5
WOMAN	3–6	7	17.5	6½	16.5	9	23
	6–9	8	20.5	7	17.5	10	25.5
	8–12	9	23	7½	19	11	28
MAN	6–8	7	17.5	7	17.5	9½	24
	8½–10	8	20.5	7½	19	10½	26.5
	10½–12	9	23	8	20.5	11	28
	12½–14	10	25.5	8½	21.5	11½	29

AVERAGE GARMENT LENGTHS

	WAIST LENGTH	HIP LENGTH	TUNIC LENGTH
CHILD	Actual body measurement	2"/5cm down from waist	6"/15cm down from waist
WOMAN	Actual body measurement	6"/15cm down from waist	11"/28cm down from waist
MEN	Men's length usually varies only 1–2"/2.5–5cm from the actual "back hip length" measurement (see Man size chart, page 149).		

GARMENT FIT

VERY-CLOSE FITTING:
Actual chest/bust measurement or less

CLOSE-FITTING:
1–2"/2.5–5cm

STANDARD-FITTING:
2–4"/5–10cm

LOOSE-FITTING:
4–6"/10–15cm

OVERSIZED:
6"/15cm or more

measurement notes

Use these mini worksheets to document the measurements of friends and family members who are muses for your design inspiration.

NAME

DATE

NAME

DATE

NAME

DATE

NAME

DATE

NAME

DATE

NAME

DATE

yarn information

Use the charts below and opposite as guides to estimating yarn amounts for the projects listed and for substituting yarns of similar weights.

SWEATERS	INFANT *16" (40cm) chest*	CHILD *24" (60cm) chest*	WOMAN *40" (100cm) chest*	MAN *48" (120cm) chest*
(2) Fine weight	500 yd (450m)	750 yd (675m)	2,100 yd (1,900m)	2,700 yd (2,400m)
(3) Light weight	400 yd (360m)	550 yd (500m)	1,600 yd (1,450 m)	2,100 yd (1,900m)
(4) Medium weight	325 yd (300m)	500 yd (450m)	1,400 yd (1,250m)	1,800 yd (1,600m)
(5) Bulky weight	250 yd (225m)	350 yd (315m)	1,000 yd (900m)	1,300 yd (1,150m)

HATS	INFANT	CHILD	WOMAN	MAN
(3) Light weight	125 yd (112m)	175 yd (160m)	225 yd (200m)	275 yd (250m)
(4) Medium weight	100 yd (90m)	150 yd (135m)	200 yd (180m)	250 yd (225m)

SOCKS	INFANT	CHILD	WOMAN	MAN
(1) Super-fine weight	125 yd (112m)	225 yd (200m)	350 yd (315m)	450 yd (405m)
(2) Fine weight	100 yd (90m)	200 yd (180m)	300 yd (270m)	400 yd (360m)

MITTENS	INFANT	CHILD	WOMAN	MAN
(3) Light weight	75 yd (66m)	100 yd (90m)	150 yd (135m)	175 yd (160m)
(4) Medium weight	50 yd (45m)	75 yd (66m)	125 yd (113m)	200 yd (180m)

GLOVES	CHILD	WOMAN	MAN
(3) Light weight	300 yd (270m)	350 yd (315m)	400 yd (360m)
(4) Medium weight	200 yd (180m)	250 yd (225m)	300 yd (270m)

YARN SUBSTITUTION

When using a different yarn than that called for in a pattern, it's crucial to match the gauge called for. It's also important to remember that patterns are designed with a certain type of yarn in mind, so factors such as drape and sheen should also be considered. For instance, if a silk yarn is called for but angora is used, even if the gauge is identical, the finished garment will differ from the original.

Yarn labels carry symbols that conform to the Craft Yarn Council's Standard Yarn Weight System, ranging from 0 (Laceweight) to 6 (Super Bulky). Many patterns use this system to indicate the weight of the recommended yarn. To substitute another yarn, find one with the same weight and knit up a swatch: determine if it yields the same gauge with the same type of feel.

standard yarn weight system

Categories of yarn, gauge ranges, and recommended needle and hook sizes

Yarn Weight Symbol & Category Names	0 Lace	1 Super Fine	2 Fine	3 Light	4 Medium	5 Bulky	6 Super Bulky
Type of Yarns in Category	Fingering 10 count crochet thread	Sock, Fingering, Baby	Sport, Baby	DK, Light Worsted	Worsted, Afghan, Aran	Chunky, Craft, Rug	Bulky, Roving
Knit Gauge Range* in Stockinette Stitch to 4 inches	33–40** sts	27–32 sts	23–26 sts	21–24 sts	16–20 sts	12–15 sts	6–11 sts
Recommended Needle in Metric Size Range	1.5–2.25 mm	2.25–3.25 mm	3.25–3.75 mm	3.75–4.5 mm	4.5–5.5 mm	5.5–8 mm	8 mm and larger
Recommended Needle U.S. Size Range	000 to 1	1 to 3	3 to 5	5 to 7	7 to 9	9 to 11	11 and larger
Crochet Gauge* Ranges in Single Crochet to 4 inch	32-42 double crochets**	21–32 sts	16–20 sts	12–17 sts	11–14 sts	8–11 sts	5–9 sts
Recommended Hook in Metric Size Range	Steel*** 1.6–1.4mm Regular hook 2.25 mm	2.25–3.5 mm	3.5–4.5 mm	4.5–5.5 mm	5.5–6.5 mm	6.5–9 mm	9 mm and larger
Recommended Hook U.S. Size Range	Steel*** 6, 7, 8 Regular hook B–1	B–1 to E–4	E–4 to 7	7 to I–9	I–9 to K–10½	K–10½ to M–13	M–13 and larger

* Guidelines only: The above reflect the most commonly used gauges and needle or hook sizes for specific yarn categories.
** Lace weight yarns are usually knitted or crocheted on larger needles and hooks to create lacy, openwork patterns. Accordingly, a gauge range is difficult to determine. Always follow the gauge stated in your pattern.
*** Steel crochet hooks are sized differently from regular hooks—the higher the number, the smaller the hook, which is the reverse of regular hook sizing.

SKILL LEVELS

When creating a design that you plan to share with other knitters, consider these skill levels from the Craft Yarn Council.

BEGINNER
Ideal first project.

EASY
Basic stitches, minimal shaping, and simple finishing.

INTERMEDIATE
For knitters with some experience. More intricate stitches, shaping, and finishing.

EXPERIENCED
For knitters able to work patterns with complicated shaping and finishing.

esperanza sweater

When creating this pullover, designer Caroline Moore envisioned a lush cowl neck and a simple yet beautiful body. For a romantic touch, she incorporated delicate cables along the borders of the body and the three-quarter sleeves as well as quiet, unobtrusive cables along the side seams.

SIZES
Sized for Small (Medium, Large). Shown in size Small.

KNITTED MEASUREMENTS
BUST
34 (37, 40)"/86.5 (94, 101.5)cm

LENGTH
20¾ (21¾, 23¼)"/52.5 (55, 59)cm

UPPER ARM
13¼ (15, 16)"/33.5 (38, 40)cm

MATERIALS
• 11 (13, 15) 1¾oz/50g balls (each approx 82yd/72m) of *Be Sweet Whipped Cream* (45% mohair/45% wool/10% silk) in Moss

• Size 7 (4.5mm) circular needles, one each 24"/60cm and 16"/40cm long, OR SIZE TO OBTAIN GAUGE

• Set (5) size 7 (4.5mm) double-pointed needles (dpns)

• Extra size 7 (4.5mm) needle to hold sts when grafting collar

• Cable needle (cn)

• 4 stitch markers (3 in one color, 1 in another)

• Size 7 (4.5mm) crochet hook for provisional cast-on

• Scrap yarn

• Yarn needle for grafting (Kitchener stitch)

GAUGE
19 sts and 25 rnds = 4"/10 cm over St st using size 7 (4.5mm) needle.
TAKE TIME TO CHECK GAUGE.

STITCH GLOSSARY
PROVISIONAL CAST-ON
Using scrap yarn and crochet hook, chain the number of sts to cast on plus a few extra. Cut a tail and pull the tail through the last chain. With knitting needle and yarn, pick up and knit the stated number of sts through the "purl bumps" on the back of the chain. To remove scrap chain, when instructed, pull out the tail from the last crochet stitch. Gently and slowly pull on the tail to unravel the crochet stitches, carefully placing each released knit stitch on a needle.

SHORT ROW WRAP AND TURN (W&T) on RS row (on WS row):
❶ Wyib (wyif), sl next st purlwise.

❷ Move yarn between the needles to the front (back).

❸ Sl the same st back to LH needle. Turn work. One st is wrapped.

❹ When working the wrapped st, insert RH needle under the wrap and work it tog with the corresponding st on needle.

KITCHENER STITCH
See instructions on page 159.

2-st LC Sl 1 st to cn and hold to *front*, k1, k1 from cn.
4-st LC Sl 2 sts to cn and hold to *front*, k2, k2 from cn.

PATTERN NOTES

Pullover is worked from the top down. The collar is worked back and forth in rows from side to side and shaped with short rows. When the collar is complete the ends are grafted together to form a tube and sts are picked up along the short edge to begin the body of the pullover, which is knit in the round.

COLLAR

Cast on 30 sts using provisional cast-on method. Do not join.

Work 16 rows in garter stitch (k every row).

*Next (short) row K20, w&t, k to end.

Next 16 rows K30.

Rep last 17 rows (short row and 16 plain rows) until piece measures 19"/38cm along the shorter side.

Cut yarn, leaving 35"/89cm tail for grafting.

Carefully undo provisional cast-on and place sts on spare needle.

Graft 2 sets of open sts tog to form tube, using Kitchener stitch method.

BODY

Pick up and k 72 sts along the short edge of the collar. Place marker (pm) of different color for beg of rnd.

K 4 rnds.

Set-up rnd K10, pm, k26, pm, k10, pm, k to end of rnd.

YOKE SHAPING

Next (inc) rnd K1, M1, [k to next marker, M1, sl marker (sm), k1, M1,] 3 times, k to last marker, M1—8 sts inc'd.

Knit 1 rnd.

Rep last 2 rnds 20 (23, 25) times more—240 (264, 280) sts.

Work even in St st (k every rnd) until yoke measures 8 (9, 9½)"/20.5 (23, 24)cm from pick-up rnd.

DIVIDE FOR BODY AND SLEEVES

Next rnd K1 *place next 50 (56, 60) sts onto scrap yarn or stitch holder for sleeve, cast on 12 (14, 16) sts,* k70 (76, 80). Rep from * to * once more, k to end, pm for new beg of rnd—164 (180, 192) sts in rnd.

Knit 1 rnd.

BEG CABLE DETAIL

Rnds 1–7 K3 (4, 5), p1, k4, p1, k76 (84, 90), p1, k4, p1, k to end.

Rnd 8 K3 (4, 5), p1, 4-st LC, p1, k76 (84, 90), p1, 4-st LC, p1, k to end.

Rep rnds 1–8 until piece measures 10 (10, 11)"/25.5 (25.5, 28)cm from underarms.

BORDER

Rnds 1–3 *K2, p2; rep from * around.

Rnd 4 *2-st LC, p2; rep from * all the way around.

Rep rnds 1–4 for 2¾"/7cm or to desired length.

Bind off loosely.

SLEEVES

(NOTE Change to dpns when sts no longer fit comfortably on circular needle.)

With shorter circular needle, pick up and k7 (8, 9) sts along underarm cast-on, pm for beg of rnd, pick up and k6 (7, 8) sts along underarm cast-on, place 50 (56, 60) sleeve stitches from scrap yarn onto needle—63 (71, 77) sts.

Work even in St st for 1 (1½, 2)"/2.5 (4, 5)cm.

Next (dec) rnd K1, ssk, k to the last 2 sts, k2tog.

Rep dec rnd every 7th rnd 6 times more—49 (57, 63) sts.

K 6 rnds.

Next (dec) rnd K1, ssk, k to end without working last k2tog—48 (56, 62) sts.

Rnds 1–3 *K2, p2; rep from * around.

Rnd 4 *2-st LC, p2; rep from * around.

Rep rnds 1–4 for 2½"/6.5cm or to desired length. Bind off loosely.

FINISHING

Weave in ends. Block to measurements.■

KITCHENER STITCH

1 Insert tapestry needle purlwise (as shown) through first stitch on front needle. Pull yarn through, leaving that stitch on knitting needle.

2 Insert tapestry needle knitwise (as shown) through first stitch on back needle. Pull yarn through, leaving stitch on knitting needle.

3 Insert tapestry needle knitwise through first stitch on front needle, slip stitch off needle and insert tapestry needle purlwise (as shown) through next stitch on front needle. Pull yarn through, leaving this stitch on needle.

4 Insert tapestry needle purlwise through first stitch on back needle. Slip stitch off needle and insert tapestry needle knitwise (as shown) through next stitch on back needle. Pull yarn through, leaving this stitch on needle. Repeat steps 3 and 4 until all stitches have been grafted. Fasten off and weave in end.

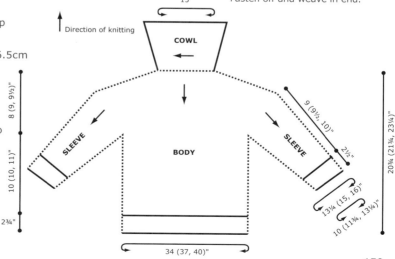

Direction of knitting

15"

COWL

SLEEVE

BODY

SLEEVE

9 (9½, 10)"

2½"

20¾ (21¾, 23¼)"

8 (9, 9½)"

10 (10, 11)"

2¾"

13¼ (15, 16)"

10 (11¾, 13¼)"

34 (37, 40)"

To my mom, Bardet Wardell, who designed the very first Be Sweet "Magic Scarf" pattern

sixth&springbooks

161 Avenue of the Americas,
New York, NY 10013
sixthandspringbooks.com

Editorial Director
JOY AQUILINO

Senior Editor
MICHELLE BREDESON

Art Director
DIANE LAMPHRON

Contributing Editor
ERIN SLONAKER

Instructions Editor
LORI STEINBERG

Schematic Illustration
ULI MONCH

Vice President, Publisher
TRISHA MALCOLM

Creative Director
JOE VIOR

Production Manager
DAVID JOINNIDES

President
ART JOINNIDES

ACKNOWLEDGMENTS
I'd like to thank three people who've helped me design and concept
this project and have supported Be Sweet from the beginning: my
sweet friend Carol Charney; the father of my child, Justin Curtis;
and my dad, John Storyk.

ABOUT THE AUTHOR
Nadine Curtis is the founder of Be Sweet, a yarn manufacturer and
distributor of knitting patterns whose mission is to offer
socially and environmentally friendly products that help support
community development and job creation programs around the
world. Be Sweet also donates a portion of its profits to
educational development programs in South Africa.
Visit Be Sweet at besweetyarns.com.

PHOTOGRAPHY AND ILLUSTRATION CREDITS
Still-life photography by Marcus Tullis.
Page 5: Sean Cope: bottom right; Sasha Gulish: top left, center left
and right; Laura Kudritzki: top right.
Illustrations: Pages 146–147: Craft Yarn Council's
YarnStandards.com; pages 145 and 159: *Vogue® Knitting* archive.

Library of Congress Control Number: 2012937686

ISBN 978-1-936096-51-0

MANUFACTURED IN CHINA

1 3 5 7 9 10 8 6 4 2